MATH MAGIC

Shape and Pattern

Written by Wendy Clemson
and David Clemson

PRINCETON ■ LONDON
www.two-canpublishing.com

Published in the United States and Canada by
Two-Can Publishing LLC
234 Nassau Street, Princeton, NJ 08542

© Two-Can Publishing 2002

For information on Two-Can books and multimedia,
call 1-609-921-6700, fax 1-609-921-3349, or visit our website
at http://www.two-canpublishing.com

Created by
act-two
346 Old Street
London EC1V 9RB

Authors: Wendy Clemson and David Clemson

Editor: Penny Smith
Designer: Helen Holmes
Illustrators: Andy Peters and Mike Stones
Photographer: Daniel Pangbourne
Prepress production: Adam Wilde

"Two-Can" is a trademark of Two-Can Publishing.
Two-Can Publishing is a division of Zenith Entertainment plc,
43-45 Dorset Street, London W1U 7NA

Hardback ISBN 1-58728-271-2
Paperback ISBN 1-58728-275-5

Hardback 1 2 3 4 5 6 7 8 9 10 03 02 01
Paperback 1 2 3 4 5 6 7 8 9 10 03 02 01

Color reproduction by the Graphic Facilities Group
Printed in Hong Kong

Contents

Seeing Shapes

Our world is full of all kinds of different shapes. Look at this picture. There are things made from curved shapes and shapes with straight sides and pointed corners. When shapes are repeated, they make fantastic patterns.

4

Find these shapes in the picture.

Can you find different colored shapes that fit together to make patterns?

5

The four-Sided family

Do all the shapes in the big picture have four sides? Shapes with four sides and four corners are called quadrilaterals. A square has sides that are all the same length and corners that match.
Try to describe the sides and corners of a rectangle.

Cut out a collection of four-sided shapes

YOU WILL NEED
paper, scissors, ruler

1 Use straight cuts to make your shapes. Try to make them different from each other, but remember, they must all have four sides.

Top tip
When you cut a square from corner to corner, each piece is exactly half.

rectangle

square

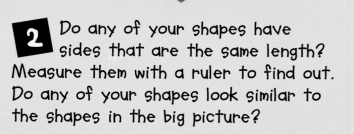

2 Do any of your shapes have sides that are the same length? Measure them with a ruler to find out. Do any of your shapes look similar to the shapes in the big picture?

BRAIN teaser

Challenge a friend to turn six squares into three by removing three toothpicks.

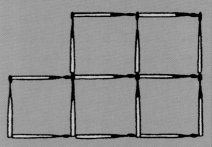

There are six squares in this shape, five small ones and one big one with four small squares inside.

Which three toothpicks will you take away to make three squares?

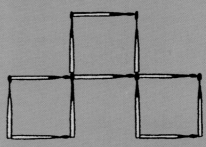

Hey presto! Now the shape has three squares.

Triangles

Do you know why a triangle is called a tri-angle? It's because tri means three and it has three corners, or angles. There are different kinds of triangles. You can have fun making triangles into pictures and new shapes with straight sides.

Make a picture from triangles

YOU WILL NEED
scissors, glue, colored paper or poster board

1 Cut out different types of triangles in all kinds of sizes and colors.

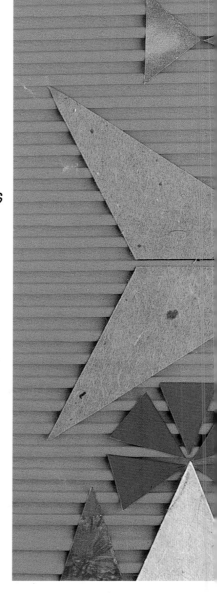

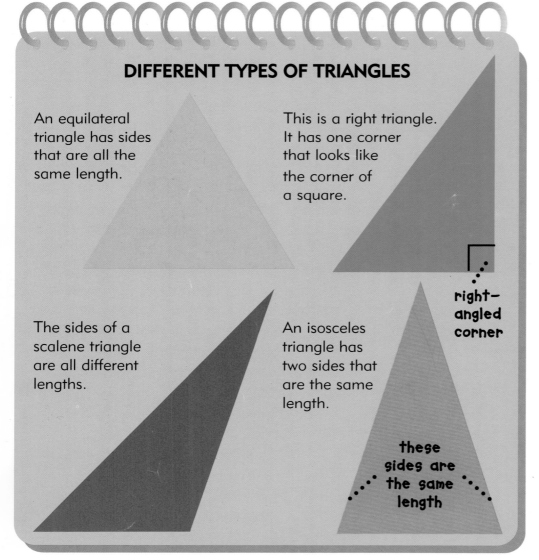

DIFFERENT TYPES OF TRIANGLES

An equilateral triangle has sides that are all the same length.

This is a right triangle. It has one corner that looks like the corner of a square.

right-angled corner

The sides of a scalene triangle are all different lengths.

An isosceles triangle has two sides that are the same length.

these sides are the same length

2 On a piece of paper or poster board, place the triangle next to each other to make a picture full of new shapes and colorful patterns. Experiment, then when you are happy with your picture, glue the triangles in place.

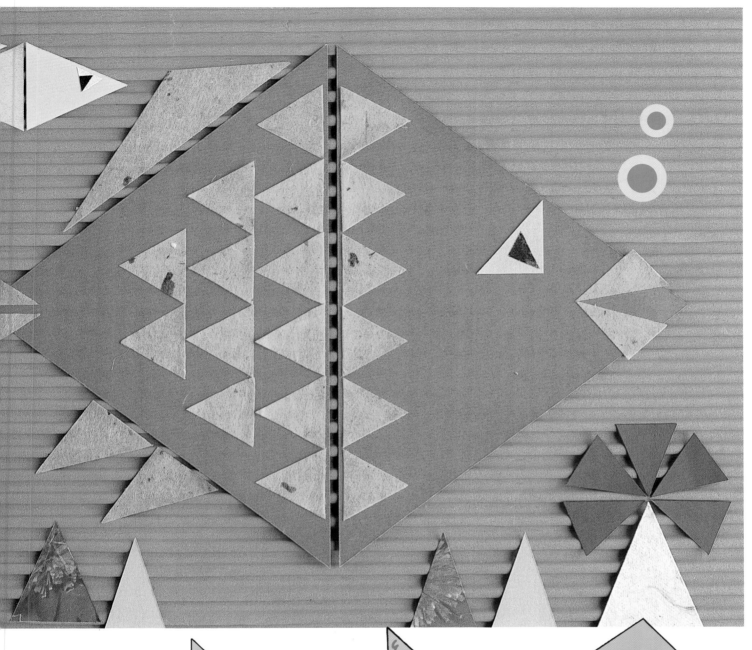

PROVE IT!

There's something magical about a right triangle. The two small corners fit exactly into the biggest corner! See for yourself.

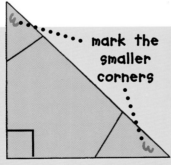

mark the smaller corners

Cut out a right triangle from the corner of a piece of paper.

Next simply cut off the marked corners.

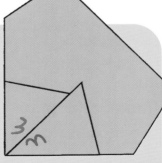

Then put them in the biggest corner. They fit perfectly!

Match That Shape

You'll be amazed at how many different shapes there are. Play this game to practice naming and matching shapes. Here's a tip. Look at the shape box below and try to remember the number of sides and matching sides of each shape.

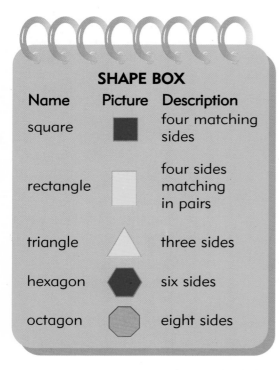

SHAPE BOX

Name	Picture	Description
square		four matching sides
rectangle		four sides matching in pairs
triangle		three sides
hexagon		six sides
octagon		eight sides

Make and play the domino game

 Make a set of 14 dominoes like the ones shown here.

YOU WILL NEED
cardboard, scissors, felt tip pens

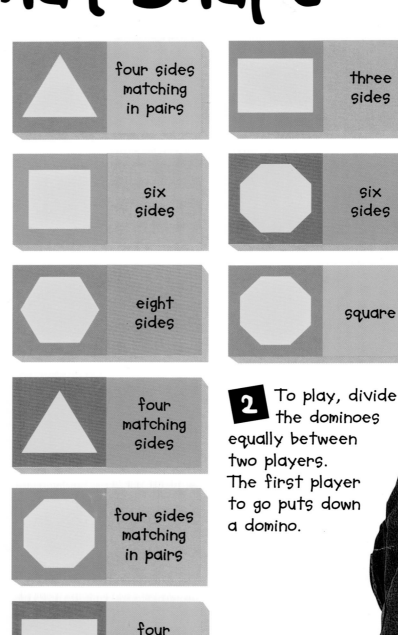

triangle — four sides matching in pairs	rectangle — three sides
square — six sides	octagon — six sides
hexagon — eight sides	octagon — square
triangle — four matching sides	
octagon — four sides matching in pairs	
rectangle — four matching sides	
hexagon — three sides	

 To play, divide the dominoes equally between two players. The first player to go puts down a domino.

10

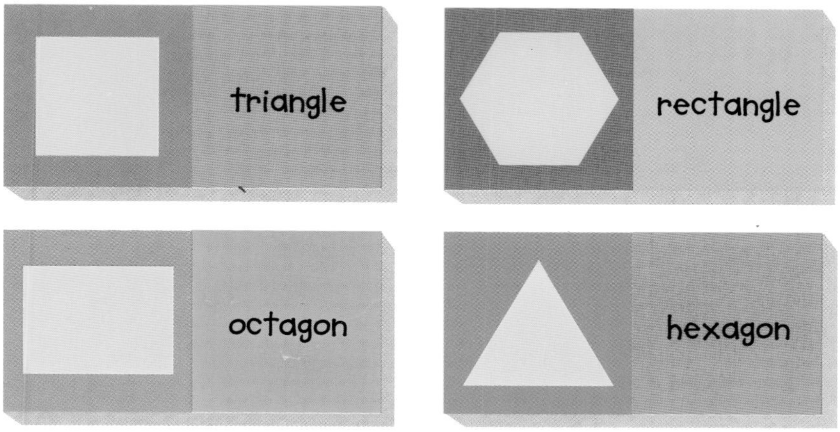

triangle

rectangle

octagon

hexagon

3 The next player matches a domino to the one on the floor. The match is by name, picture, or description. Take turns. The player left with the fewest dominoes is the winner.

Now try this

BRAIN teaser

Here's a chance to show star quality! Challenge a friend to make one five-sided shape, called a pentagon, inside another.

First draw a pentagon, then draw a line from one corner to another.

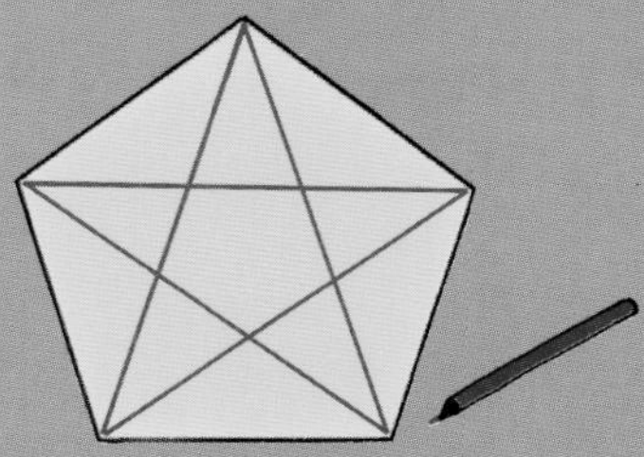

Now join all the other corners. Here's your star, but what else can you see? There's a new pentagon in the center!

three sides

six sides

square

eight sides

six sides

octagon

four sides matching in pairs

four matching sides

oblong

Turning Around

As time passes, the hands on a clock turn in one direction. This is called clockwise. If time could go backward, the hands would turn the other way. This direction is counterclockwise. A spiral is also a kind of turn. It starts in the middle and turns further and further away from where it started.

clockwise

counterclockwise

Wow!
Water drains out of your bath in a counterclockwise direction. But if you were in Australia, it would drain clockwise!

Decorate cakes with spiral patterns

1 Pipe writing icing in spirals on cupcakes. Start in the middle. On one cake, make the spiral clockwise. On another cake, make it counterclockwise.

YOU WILL NEED
ready-to-use writing icing, cakes, sweets

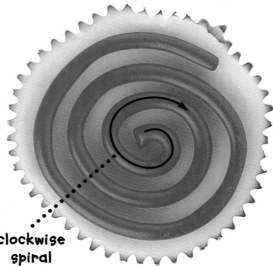
clockwise spiral

counterclockwise spiral

PROVE IT!

The edge of a circle is the same distance from the center all the way around. To check, draw a circle. Fold it in half and half again, then unfold it. The center is where the fold lines cross. Now measure.

2 Decorate a big cake with colorful spirals and candies. Practice on paper first. What pictures are you going to make?

13

Right Angles

When you spin all the way round on your feet, you make a complete turn and end up where you started. But when you move in a quarter turn, you change direction. A right angle is a quarter turn. There are four right angles in a square, one at each corner.

Top tip

Make a right-angle tester to check the angles in your maze. Fold a piece of paper, or even a leaf, in half. Then fold it again so the first fold lines up.

Make a right-angled maze

1 Cut out at least 24 squares of paper. The squares should all have $2\frac{1}{2}$ in. (6 cm) sides.

> **YOU WILL NEED**
> scissors, paper, colored tape

2 Make guide lines by folding each square in half, then half again. Unfold the squares. Use colored tape to copy the patterns shown at the top of the next page. Use your guide lines to position the tape accurately.

PROVE IT!

To make a complete turn, you have to turn through four right angles, or quarter turns. In the picture, how many times has the man changed direction? What shape is he making?

start here

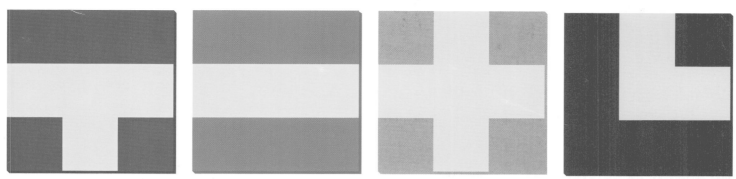

Copy the patterns on these squares

3 Now lay out your squares so the colored tape makes roads in the maze. Trace a finger around the maze. How many right angled turns can you make?

Now try this

BRAIN teaser

Challenge friends to see how many right triangles they can make from one rectangle.

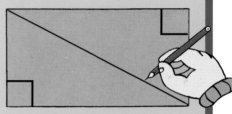

One way is to draw a line like this. Now there are two right triangles.

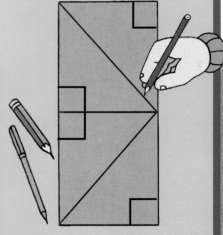

A better way is to draw three lines. This makes four right triangles.

15

fold and cut

What happens when you fold a piece of paper in half then cut a shape on the fold? Experiment with fold and cut shapes to find out. Before you open them out, think how they will look. Are they the same or different to how you imagined?

Cut out folded shapes

YOU WILL NEED

paper, scissors

1 Fold a sheet of paper and make a single cut across the two layers. Open the paper. What shape do you have? Now try making two, three, and four cuts. What shapes have you cut out?

2 These shapes have been cut out. Which pieces of cut paper belong together?

Now try this

BRAIN teaser

Challenge a friend to make a paper man into eight men!

fold ....

.... outer edges

.....outer edges

folds

First, fold a thin piece of square paper in half, then fold it in half again to make a smaller square.

Next, fold the paper from corner to corner. Make sure that the outer edges are all together.

Now draw a picture of just one man. His arms and legs must reach right to the folds in the paper.

PROVE IT!

A shape cut from folded paper is the same on both sides of the fold. Is this true? Look where the fold lines are on the shapes below. Three of the shapes are made from folded paper. One is not.

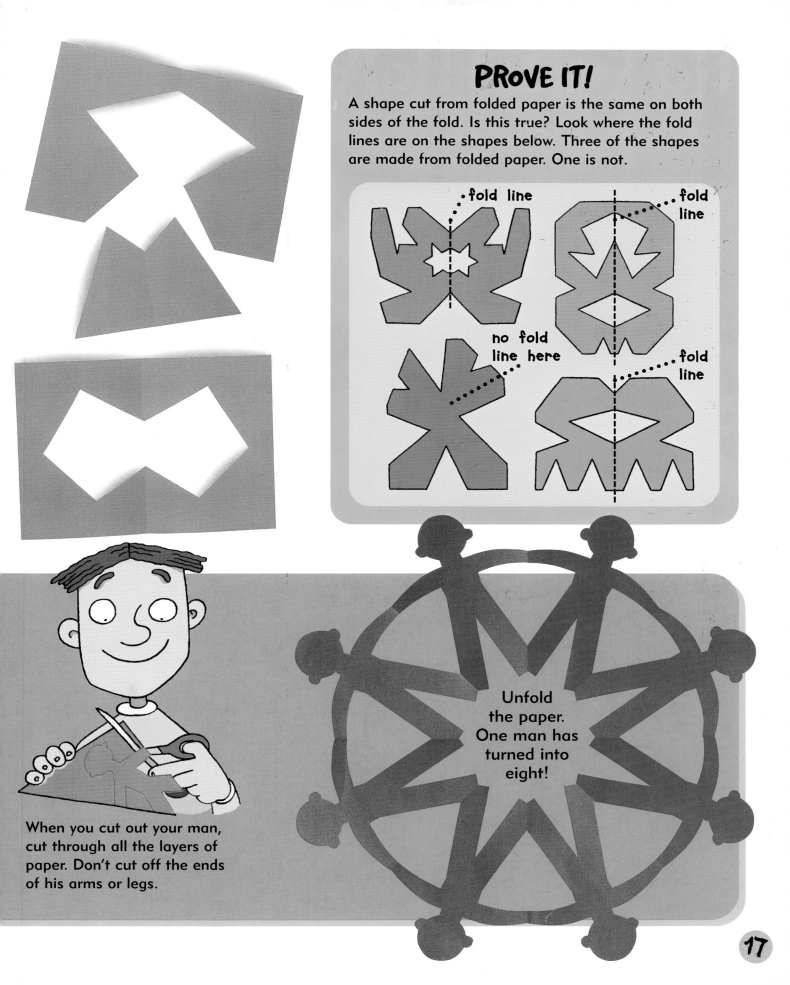

fold line

fold line

no fold line here

fold line

When you cut out your man, cut through all the layers of paper. Don't cut off the ends of his arms or legs.

Unfold the paper. One man has turned into eight!

Half and Half

Look at the big shark. A fold line divides it into two halves that match exactly. This is called the line of symmetry. Check that both halves of the shark are the same. Count the number of teeth, eyes, and fins in each half.

line of symmetry

Make a symmetrical card

YOU WILL NEED
poster board, pencil, scissors, glue

1 Fold a piece of poster board in half. Draw half a picture right up to the fold line.

2 Cut out your poster board and make sure it will stand up. Then write your message on the back.

Now try this
BRAIN teaser

Challenge a friend to double the number of cookies on a plate. Here's how to make it work.

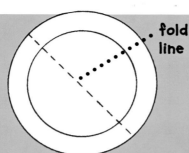

fold line

First draw a picture of a plate and cut it out. Fold the plate in half, then unfold it.

Draw and color in a handful of cookies on one side of the fold.

Hold a mirror along the fold. Now you can see twice the number of cookies than you had before!

3 Make up your own symmetrical picture cards. Decorate them with colored shapes and patterns.

PROVE IT!

A shape can have more than one line of symmetry. The top pictures have several, while the middle pictures have one each. Prove this by holding a mirror along the lines to see if the reflections match. The bottom pictures have no lines of symmetry.

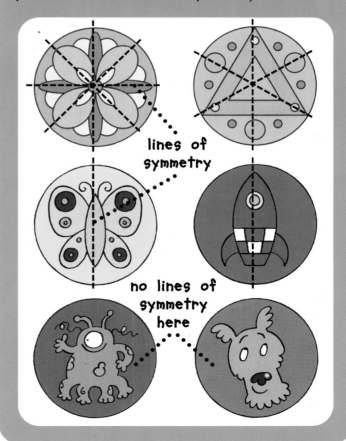

lines of symmetry

no lines of symmetry here

Pin Pictures

Everything you see has a shape. Many shapes have straight sides. Make your own shapes and patterns with yarn or string and a pinboard. How many different shapes can you make?

Make and use a pinboard

YOU WILL NEED
ruler, pencil, styrofoam, push pins, yarn, or string

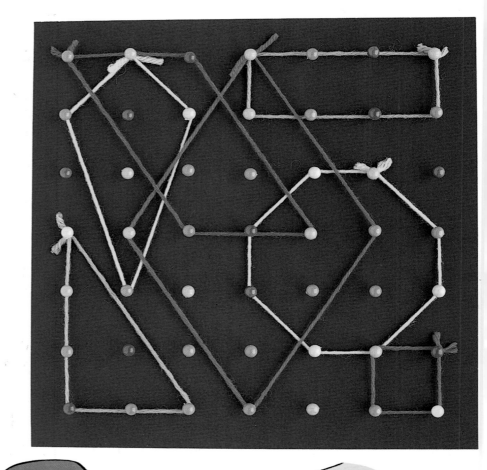

1 Draw a grid of squares on thick styrofoam with about six squares along each side. The squares should measure about 1 in. by 1 in. (3 cm by 3 cm.).

2 The next part is tricky, so ask an adult to help. Push pins through the corners of the squares. Make sure the pins are securely in place.

3 Knot the yarn around one pin and wind it around others to make a shape. Tie a knot. Make as many shapes as you can.

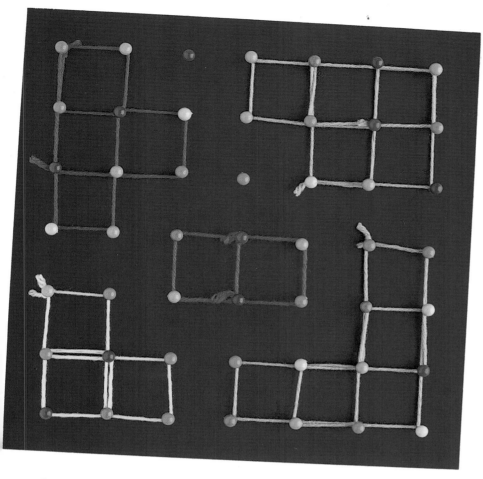

4 Now make patterns of squares that touch along at least one side. Try making these using two, three, four, and five squares.

PROVE IT!

These patterns are made up of four squares that touch along at least one side. You can make five different patterns this way. Four are shown here. The fifth is on the pinboard above. Can you find it?

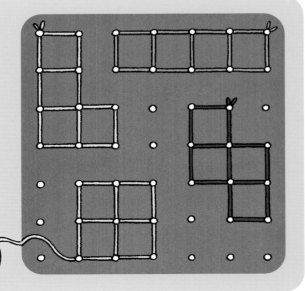

BRAIN teaser

Wind yarn around any square on your pinboard. The number of pins inside the square is a square number. Challenge a friend to work out some square numbers.

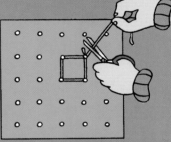

First get your friend to wind yarn around four pins to make a small square. This shows that four is a square number.

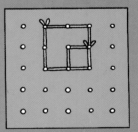

What is the next square number? Count the pins and you will see that it is nine.

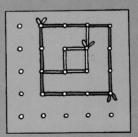

What about the next one? This square number is 16. Use your pinboard to figure out more square numbers.

Three Dimensions

A flat shape, such as a square, has length and width. The sides show two dimensions. A cube, or square box, has three dimensions.
It has length, width, and height.
Make a cube from an arrangement of flat squares, called a net.

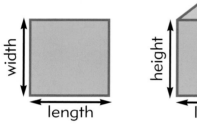

Make and decorate a cube picture box

YOU WILL NEED
index cardboard, ruler, pencil, scissors, tape, photographs, glue

1 On the cardboard, draw a square with sides of about 3 in. (8 cm.). Cut it out. Copy the pattern shown below by drawing around your cut-out square. Make sure the squares in the pattern touch.

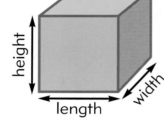

PROVE IT!

On this page, there are five different ways to arrange your squares to make a net for a cube. Can you see them? To make sure that each net works, copy it, cut it out, and make it into a little box.

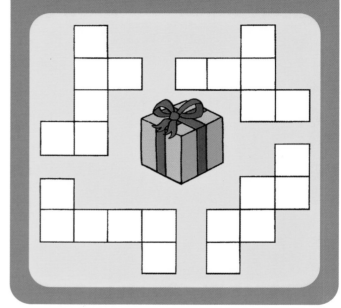

2 Now cut around the outside of the shape.

Top tip

A dice is a cube. It has six faces, or flat surfaces. This is easy to remember because the greatest number is six.

3 Fold the shape along the lines of the squares to make a cube. Tape the cube together.

4 Cut your favourite photographs to size, then stick them to the faces of the cube.

Cylinders and Cones

Shapes with curved surfaces roll. The surface of a round ball, or sphere, is completely curved. Cones and cylinders also have curved surfaces, but they have flat faces, too, which means they can stand upright. Cylinders and cones are the perfect shapes to make a space rocket pencil holder.

Wow!
Any slice across a sphere has a circular face, but not all the faces are the same size.

Make and decorate a pencil holder

YOU WILL NEED
empty paper towel roll, ruler, scissors, colored poster board, glue, tape, felt tip pen

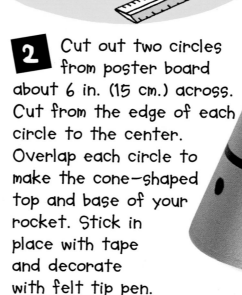

1 First cut the empty paper towel roll to size, it should be about 7 in. (18 cm.) long. Cut a piece of poster board large enough to cover it. Glue this over the paper towel roll, then decorate it to look like a rocket.

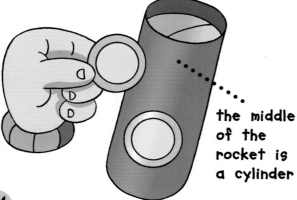

the middle of the rocket is a cylinder

2 Cut out two circles from poster board about 6 in. (15 cm.) across. Cut from the edge of each circle to the center. Overlap each circle to make the cone-shaped top and base of your rocket. Stick in place with tape and decorate with felt tip pen.

the rocket top is cone shaped

3 To make the wings cut out another circle of poster board about 4 in. (10 cm.) across. Fold it in half. Cut slits in the rocket as shown in the picture. Push the wings into the slits.

cut one slit here

cut one slit here

4 Stand your rocket on its base. Use tape to hold it in position. Place pens inside it and put on the rocket top!

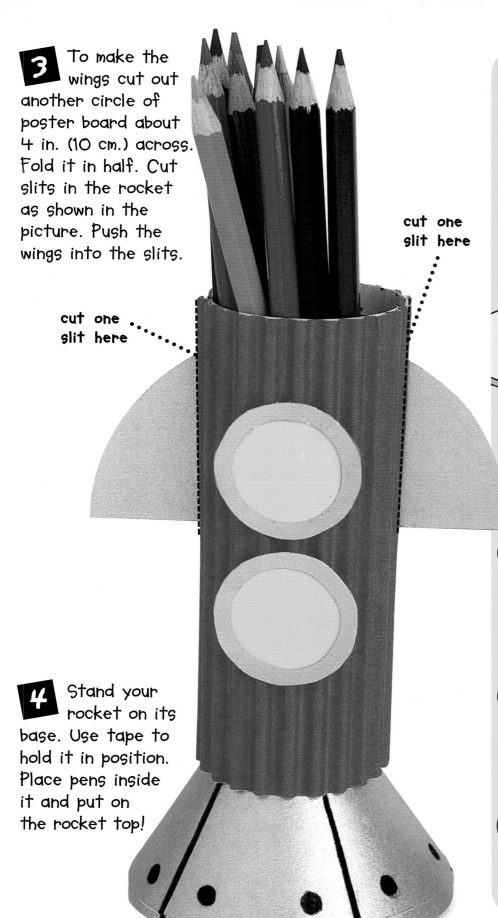

Now try this

BRAIN teaser

Challenge a friend to guess what shapes you will make when you slice up a cylinder.

First make a sausage shape from clay. Cut off the ends to make a cylinder.

cut here

Make the cut shown above. What shape is the cut face? The answer is a circle.

cut here

What shape is the cut face this time? The answer is an ellipse.

cut here

Now what shape is the cut face? The answer is a rectangle.

Finding Grid References

It can be tricky finding your way around a town. Maps help because they show a big area as a small picture. On this map there is a grid of crisscrossing lines. Each square between the lines has a letter and a number. This gives a square its own name, such as A1 or C4.

Finding a grid reference

First find the ice cream shop on the map. (It's at the bottom, by the red car.) Next, find the letter at the base of the column, beneath the ice cream shop. It is B. Now find the number of the row alongside the ice cream shop. It is 1. So the ice cream shop is at B1.

 Check out these grid references.

D6   C6

 Now find the grid references for these places on the map.

bus stop

coffee shop   school   flower shop

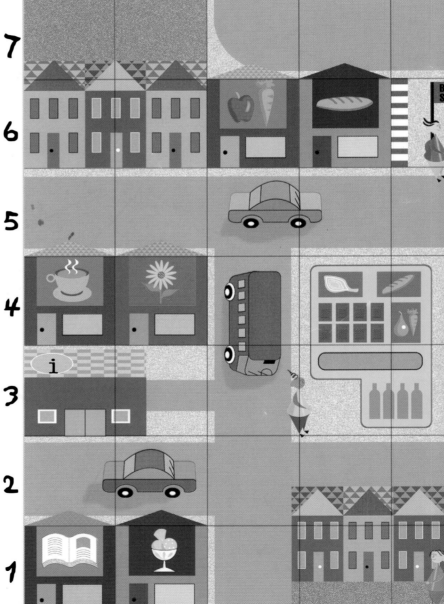

26

Now try this
BRAIN teaser

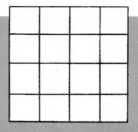

Challenge a friend to copy and double the size of a picture using a grid. Here's how to do it.

First draw a grid on tracing paper. Tape it over the picture you want to copy.

Draw a second grid on ordinary paper. This should be twice the size of the first grid.

Now for the clever part, carefully copy the picture onto the larger grid, square by square.

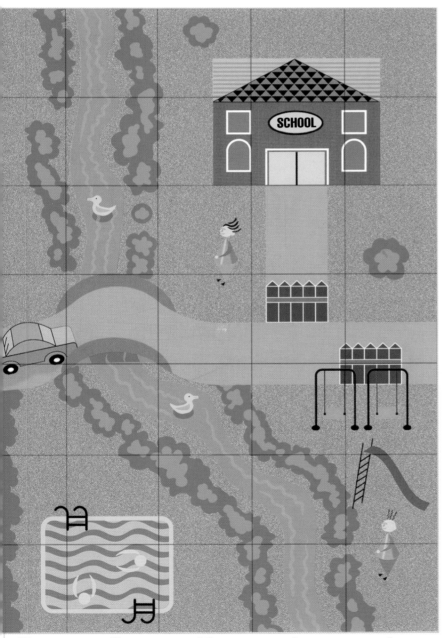

F   G   H   I   J

PROVE IT!

When you have a grid reference, as well as a grid, you can find what you are looking for.

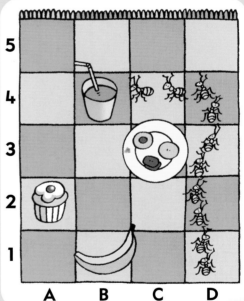

This is a grid of a picnic table. Look at grid reference B4. You'll find a drink there. But watch out for grid references beginning with D. Can you see why?

Compass Points

North, south, east, and west are the points on a compass that help you find your way. On a compass, a magnetic needle always points north, so you can find the other directions. Play this treasure hunt game. Look at the compass to check you're moving in the right direction.

NORTH

WEST

EAST

SOUTH

Hunt the treasure game

YOU WILL NEED
ruler, scissors, index card, pencil, colored pieces, small coin

1 For this game you will have to make a spinner, so cut out a 3 in. (7 cm.) square of the card. Decorate it as shown. Push a pencil through the center of your spinner.

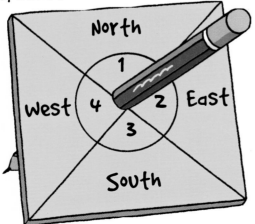

HOW TO PLAY

◆ This is a game for two to four players.

◆ First, put the treasure, which is the coin, on one of the four islands. This is now the treasure island.

◆ Now, each player choose a different colored piece. Put the pieces on Central Harbor.

◆ Take turns spinning the spinner. Spin it once to find the direction to move in, then again to see how many squares to cross.

◆ When you can't follow the spinner's directions exactly, you can't move your counter until your next turn.

◆ The first player to land on treasure island is the winner!

Get back on course go one square south then two squares east

Mermaid sin directions to go one squar east then on square sout

Lost in a storm go back to Central Harbor

Message in a bottle go three squares eas

Get back on course go three squares east

Dolphin show you the wa go one square sout

Carried by a tidal wave to Pineapple Island

Mermaid sin directions to go one squar east then on square nort

Get back on course go one square north then two squares east

Carried by tidal wave to Mango Island		Get back on course go three squares south		Lost in a storm go back to Central Harbor	Get back on course go one square south then two squares west
	Dolphin shows you the way go one square south		Message in a bottle go three squares south	Mermaid sings directions to you go one square west then one square south	
COCONUT ISLAND		Hit jagged rocks miss a turn	PINEAPPLE ISLAND		Carried by a tidal wave to Banana Island
	Bitten by a shark miss a turn	Dolphin shows you the way go one square north		Lost in a storm go back to Central Harbor	
Carried by a tidal wave to Pineapple Island		START HERE CENTRAL HARBOR	Carried by a tidal wave to Banana Island		Get back on course go three squares west
	Message in a bottle go three squares north	Bitten by a shark miss a turn		Message in a bottle go three squares west	
BANANA ISLAND	Hit jagged rocks miss a turn		MANGO ISLAND		Lost in a storm go back to Central Harbor
	Message in a bottle go three squares east	Dolphin shows you the way go one square north		Mermaid sings directions to you go one square west then one square north	
Lost in a storm go back to Central Harbor	Get back on course go three squares north		Carried by a tidal wave to Coconut Island		Get back on course go one square north then two squares west

29

Useful Words

angle
An angle is part of a complete turn. It is made where two straight lines meet.

angle

clockwise
This is when something moves around in the same direction as the hands on a clock.

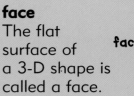

face
The flat surface of a 3-D shape is called a face.

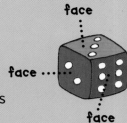

face

face

face

counterclockwise
This is when something moves around in the opposite direction of the hands on a clock.

compass points
The main compass points are north, south, east, and west. They help travelers find their way.

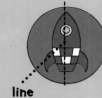

line of symmetry
A shape with exactly matching halves has a line of symmetry.

line of symmetry

Name That Shape

circle
This shape has one curved edge. Every place on its outline is the same distance from the center.

triangle
This shape has three straight sides that are all the same length. Other triangles have two sides the same length or all sides that are different lengths.

square

This 2-D shape has four equal sides and four equal corners.

rectangle
This is a 2-D shape with two matching long sides, two matching short sides, and four matching corners.

star

This straight-sided 2-D shape is called a star.

pentagon

This is a 2-D shape with five straight sides.

hexagon

A hexagon is a 2-D shape with six straight sides.

octagon
This is a 2-D shape with eight straight sides.

ellipse
This oval shape looks like a flattened circle.

cone

This 3-D shape has a flat face that is a circle and a curved surface that ends in a point.

cylinder
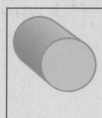
This 3-D shape has two faces that are circles and one curved surface.

right angle

A right angle is a quarter of a complete turn. The corner of a square forms a right angle.

right angle

spiral

A spiral is a turn that winds farther and farther away from its starting point.

three dimensions (3-D)

Solid and hollow shapes are 3-D. They have three dimensions, length, width, and height.

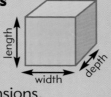

length
width
depth

two dimensions (2-D)

Flat shapes are 2-D. They have only two dimensions, length and width.

length
width

---

cube
This is a 3-D shape with six square faces.

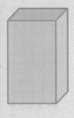

rectangular prism
This shape has six faces. They can all be rectangles. Or a rectangular prism can have two square faces and four rectangle faces.

pyramid
This shape has triangular faces that meet at a point. Its base can be any straight sided shape.

prism
The faces at the ends of a prism are exactly the same shape, size, and distance apart along all sides. The end faces are joined together by rectangles.

triangular prism

hexagonal prism

sphere
This 3-D shape has one curved face and looks like a perfectly round ball.

Index

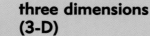

Notes for Parents and Teachers

This book is intended to help children become confident at recognizing and making shapes and patterns. It also helps children to understand directions. Whenever we pack a lunchbox, choose a screwdriver, or walk around shops, we use our knowledge about shape, pattern, place, and direction.

Shape

Our world is three dimensional. Even sheets of paper and paint on a wall have thickness or depth. Young children learn about shapes from the world around them. Help them build on this knowledge in the following ways:

- Look at and name shapes in your neighborhood. What shape is a front door or a traffic cone?

- Discuss how shapes are appropriate for their use. A roof is often in the shape of a prism so that water flows off it easily. A broom handle is cylindrical. Its smooth surface makes it comfortable to hold. A triangle is a strong shape that's useful for holding up a heavy object such as a bridge.

- Encourage children to describe irregular shapes such as shells or rocks.

Pattern

A pattern is made by repeating shapes. When children make patterns, they learn about balance and symmetry. They also learn to predict how things will look. All these skills are useful for an understanding of art, design, and technology.

- Help your child to find examples of symmetry in nature. Point out the broad symmetry and pattern in flowers, leaves, insects, and snowflakes.

- Look closely for patterns in real life. Is there a pattern on your curtains or kitchen floor? See how many shapes they are made from and how the shapes fit together.

- Help children make up their own patterns when they decorate cards or make wrapping paper.

Place and direction

Understanding the direction of a turn, either clockwise or counterclockwise, is the first step towards locating a place. The next steps are following compass directions and simple map reading. Here are ways to guide children:

- Look at local maps with children. Ask them to find their homes and schools.

- What's the shortest way to the park or zoo?

Praise and encourage

The most important thing is to not make maths seem like a chore. Show children math is part of the everyday world, an important life skill, and that it can be fun. Encourage children to work hard and praise the work they do. Then you'll help them have a positive approach to learning.